Anna Saunders

The Prohibition of Touch

Indigo Dreams Publishing

First Edition: The Prohibition of Touch
First published in Great Britain in 2022 by:
Indigo Dreams Publishing
24, Forest Houses
Cookworthy Moor
Halwill
Beaworthy
Devon
EX21 5UU

www.indigodreamspublishing.com

Anna Saunders has asserted her right under the Copyright, Designs and Patents Act 1988 to be identified as the author of this work.

ISBN 978-1-912876-72-3

British Library Cataloguing in Publication Data. A CIP record for this book can be obtained from the British Library.

Designed and typeset in Palatino Linotype by Indigo Dreams. Cover design by Jason Conway, Daydream Academy, from artwork by Sarah-Jane Crowson.
Printed and bound in Great Britain by 4edge Ltd.

Papers used by Indigo Dreams are recyclable products made from wood grown in sustainable forests following the guidance of the Forest Stewardship Council.

To Francis, with much love and gratitude.

Acknowledgements

With heartfelt thanks to Dawn Gorman, Zoe Brooks, Josephine Lay, Clair Chilvers and Kate and Sheila Saunders for their invaluable and empathic feedback and acute editorial advice.

To the magazines and journals that believed in my work, in particular the following editors and poets Charley Barnes, Catrice Greer, Nigel Kent, Matthew MC Smith, Chase Dimock, Helen Ivory, Robert Frede Kenter, Isabelle Kenyon, Stuart Bancroft and Lois Hambleton.

Poems from this collection have been published in the following ezines and journals; *Icefloe, An Invitation to Love, The 6ress, Ink Sweat and Tears, High Window, Anthropocene, Boats Against the Grain, Marble Poetry, Dear Reader, As it Ought to Be, Black Nore Review, Allegro, Finished Creatures.*

Additional thanks go to the poetry community who have attended my readings and inspired me with their poems.

And to the wonderful King and Queen of Poetry: Dawn Bauling and Ronnie Goodyer, for their faith in my poetry and unwavering support.

Foreword

The power of physical contact is a constant theme in this startling new collection by Anna Saunders. *The Prohibition of Touch* is populated with vivid characters from myth, legend and real life, all of whom understand the impact of intimacy or its lack.

Here we meet a bereaved woman as she consults the goddess of Loneliness, a girl who 'stockpiles memories of touch', Pasiphae, whose taboo encounter with the bull spawns a monster, an arsonist's wife who dreams of a wedding dress made of fire, the moon as it tries to teach a girl how to gain a new skin to recover from an attack, a man who crafts a lover from wool, and a mother and daughter, walking in mist, whose closeness means that even 'At the heart of the Fret, the day is full of diamonds.'

Here are poems, at times celebratory, at others elegiac or angry, that meet the readers eye and offer solace, despite the fact they sometimes sing of the dark —just like the White Hart in the city park whose gentle gaze says 'that all is well, that the signs are still auspicious/despite, despite'.

CONTENTS

The Prohibition of Touch

Pasiphaë's Confession

Forgive me Father,
Eros kicked in my door as I slept.

I dreamt of flanks gleaming
like wet stone,
the suede nap of nose.

Father, I ran to Daedalus.
He used oak, mahogany,
built a wooden cow
bade me clamber into it
so the ox would think I was one of its own.

A sailor brought the rope,
looped it through the bull's nose-ring,
pulled him to me.

I was fragrant with vanilla oils.
As if it mattered how I smelt.

All night the violins were played
to drown out the sounds.

Father, the wood still stands firm,
and in the bed he built,
I swell like a pomegranate.

One day Daedalus will construct a maze
in which to entrap my hoofed son.

But first he brought the wooden beast
for me to enter into,

as if lust meant hunkering
in the emptiness
of an animal's heart.

A Riddle

Love I sit
Love I stand
Love I hold
Fast in Hand
I see Love
but Love sees not me.

Golden boy, when I stroked you,
your back had the warmth of hay in sun.

Without words you lolled against me.
Your eyes, molten, asked something
that I could not translate.

I wanted you to lie only with me,
glistening snout against my skin.
To keep you near I would feed you titbits.

You came to heel once, for a short while,
kept close, pressed against me
like a rug to a bare floor.

They say I may be hanged.
Beauty and birth will not save me
but guile will.
I ask everyone to solve my riddle.

Oh Love, my hands are warmed under your pelt.
My toes are cushioned in your fur.
I wear you like a house wears a haunting.

The Gold Ring

All the stories begin the same,
the Beautiful Girl lost in the Dark Forest
having strayed too far from the path
that should lead her safely
from mother to other, from hearth to hearth.

The Beautiful Girl walking into the forest
where, startled
by the knife glint of moon,

she goes deeper and deeper,
until she loses her way and
runs to the door of a man
whose smile she misunderstands.

There is so much I would teach her
if only she would listen,
but my voice is drowned out
by the man's entreaties.

Here's my trick,
dangle a ring in the air before her
so the glint leads her back
through the woods.
She will follow the cold gold
back home.

Sometimes I question my magic.
Why bring her out of the woods,
to a house where her mother
has a husband waiting, scuttling his hooves
like a bridled horse, hot breath
pluming in the air?

The Painted Hare

Hare, hare, god send thee care/I am in hare's likeness just now/
But I shall be in a woman's likeness even now.

When we dig her up she is sleek as porcelain
but covered in flowers, head turned to one side,
as if listening for the guns.

I tell my man not to laugh or call her *bunny,*
she is a hare, or half woman, half animal,
and her body contains all of time –
black on her spine for night,
white on her front for the new day.

He wants to clean her under the tap
as soon as he has hauled her out,
but I say *brush the earth off gently*
leave some on to keep her whole,
she comes from below
and this soiled air could destroy her.

I could use her as a mirror, her glaze
has such a sheen
and she is curved like me, cracked
by heavy handling.

He called me *crazy* again the other night,
slapped me when I cried,
hit me as I begged him not to go out hunting,

But that is me
that you have your sights on,
I say, long-eared and leaping,
trying to outrun my own death.

An Alchemy

Last time I walked here,
the thistles were veiled
with webs, a hundred spiked brides,
their filigree sequined with rain.

Now they are bound with the springs
and spindles
of the rough brother of clematis,
Old Man's Beard,
who crept his way up,
predated on every slender vine.

I created this gold season
of gilded death,
the leaves' molten exodus,
their gold flight through air.

Even wind does my bidding,
its choir sings a slow dirge
to which the clouds
troupe cross a cloistered sky.

The man who took my Persephone
wasn't the only one to abduct a girl

every year countless Hades
rip daughters from the earth.
The trees grieve all season.

Hell in flesh, these Hades,
yet they cannot outdo the alchemy.

Even at this time of loss
there is such splendour.

Look to the boughs
where my autumn colours reside
next to a lost daughter's green.

I ask Loneliness, *What place is this?*

She says
Be you of fire or of water
all elements end up here.

All summer he swam across to me.
I watched from my tower,
burning my lamp all night, lighthouse
and lodestone for his crossing.

He breasted the waves for love,
pale face breaking above the waters,
curls light as spume.

That was summer, my skin was golden
as sand; the low-slung moon gave him light
to navigate by.

All the night I held aloft a contained flame,
it danced in its captivity
as he rode the rearing back of the sea.

Distance is at first desire,
and then later, a barrier.
I wondered how he would get to me.

In winter, I grew cold,
my candle blown out by my sighs.
Love was drowned for lack of light.

Now my boy is washed up on the rock
limp as bladderwrack.

I ask Loneliness – *where is this*?
The darkness resembles my tower.

She says, *this is the place you arrive at*
when love cannot find its way home.

After Echo

This is form calling on absence,
emptiness crying back to the flesh.

Come here, come here, you call.
Come here, come here, he shouts back.

You followed fast on his heels like a shadow,
waited till he broke from another chase.
Now he senses something of you,
hears your paw-soft tread.

Come here, come here, you call.
Come here, come here, he shouts back.

Didn't *Love* curse you once,
make your tongue a slave?
The wound you received is a cavern
in which sound repeats.

Come here, come here, you call.
Come here, come here, he shouts back.

When you emerge from the bushes
into the bright light, the hunter will recoil.
Stay in the darkness, lady,
he loves his own shadow alone.

This is form calling on absence
emptiness crying back to the flesh.

Come here, come here, you call.
Come here, come here, he shouts back.

Lockdown Rapunzel Lets Down Her Hair

Through a stone window slit
the world resembles a single tear.

I bought silk to splice my braids
but you cannot make a ladder from hair.

I dreamt how men unravelled in front of me,
how disease grew wild
and families split and splintered.

History will untangle why we were up here.
Men let us down, like unpinned hair.

You cannot make a rope from gold,
or a ladder from money.

My lockdown tresses fall to nothing.

History will untangle why we were up here.
Men let us down like unpinned hair.

The Prohibition of Touch

Recently I have been thinking about prohibition –
how the poor made moonshine, bathtub gin,
while the wealthy crammed their cellars with fine malts.

That's what happens when you criminalise desire,
it goes underground, or only the rich get the silk of it.

Through my window I watch a man holding a girl.
Two months of isolation and skin hunger,
yet the already-coupled are well fed.

At those parties they slaked their thirst
with rough liquor – the fire of it incinerating thought.

What happens now as we outlaw lips,
ban embraces -where does all the contraband go?

I have been dreaming vividly during lockdown,
my mask-less mouth all nerve and chemical cocktail,

as I slug back memories of touch that I have stockpiled
in an illicit underground dive called *Sleep*.

That Summer

we bleached our sinks to palimpsests
washed our letters
until their words bled out.

We deified food,
iconised oranges,
saw white sliced bread as holy leaf.

That summer
we were pulled from the packs
or forced to hunker in hides.

Acts of intimacy were outlawed,
and we horded memories of touch.

And as the days grew longer (for the lucky)
we shared pictures of rivers turned translucent,
wild boar walking single file
through city streets,
goats lazily nibbling privet hedges

or blue skies,
a single cloud half-covering a blood-orange sun

like a medic's mask
eclipsing
a savagely scoured face.

The sirens   *The Sirens*

Is this a child's howl? It rises and repeats insistently.

> *You must listen out for The Sirens, steer your ship from them.*

A sea of cars parts as the ambulances come through. Wail, yelp and
phaser, their echoing song.

> *Muses of the lower world,*
> *their music begins in windless calm,*
> *ends in tempest.*

Notes almost too high for the human ear, a pitch that could shatter
glass.

> *They lap at souls, a tidal dosing, immersive as opiates.*

Lucky you, if you hear the sirens, the claxon is as remote to those
cocooned in coma as the gull's harsh caw is to a drowned man.

> *Blessed are you, if you hear the Sirens, their victims,*
> *borne along in Poseidon's cart,*
> *no longer hear the dark Air.*

Unlucky those whose wrecks are accompanied by the metal-
throated song.

Some are already all salt, *all spirit – light and lithe as spume.*

The Hall of the Chosen Dead has Many Doors

All the doors to the Hall are identical,
though the battlefields from where you came
are various.

Some of you have waged war in ice, some fire,
some of you have fought in deep waters,
mute as fish, your screams sealed in blue,
but the doors through which you enter are identical.

You have been chosen for your bravery.
You will feast here.

The sacred boar is boiled for you, it is the best of bacons:
you will pluck the flesh like petals
from a rose, swallow it as easily as oysters.

Each night the boar is killed for you, and in the morning it is reborn.

All the doors look identical but you, The Chosen Dead,
will bring the ephemera of your different paths.

Some of you will carry stones in your shoes,
some will shake off snow,
some will wear the oceans, your hair as slick and glistening as seaweed.

You have been chosen for your bravery.
This is how we reward you
by kissing life back into the beast so we can kill it again for you.

To the Gods, the viscera, the fat
to you, our Chosen Dead, the plump, sweet flesh ,
the honeyed blood,
the body raised from the dead and offered to you.

.

Ask yourself this before you deny me Avernus

Didn't I honour *Dark Night* with my altar?

What did Orpheus have that I can't replace with a pen?

If Theseus and Hercules could go down, why not I?

Didn't I please Pluto, draping my flesh
across the altar?

Wasn't I the one who was always on fire,
didn't I cauterise the night?

Aren't I already lost, and don't fear
the entangled paths?

Haven't I swung my sword at phantasms,
run through airy thoughts with my blade?

Haven't I tried to murder a mind full of monsters?

Haven't I learnt a thousand different ways of dying?

Didn't I see the boat leave, its wood creaking
with the weight of my thousand dead?

An Ancestor of Odin

Thought and *Memory*
rise above the battlefield of his life,
the two ravens fly from him to the slain.

Raw, Raw, Raw –
each growl torn from the deep.

Dark angels that once fed flesh to Elijah
now they soar above him
as he counts the dead;

the foxes pestled to a paste
by tyres, the insects poisoned
by pesticides, the gulls bloated
with plastics, the butterflies
that starve upon the lawn.

Raw, Raw, Raw —
each growl torn from the deep.

The grief is too much,
his voice is lacerated
as he cries of those who destroy
the earth's alchemy.

Raw, Raw, Raw,
each growl torn from the deep.

The Wild Hunt

You who

sleep spooned,
Siamese-twinned with your latest love,
slip under, fingers scrolling a screen,
eclipsed by clouds of red,
brought down by barbiturates,

felled
by family, work,
or are too fatigued,
too intoxicated, too aroused,

you will not see it.

You who

wake to a low rumble,
then burrow back under,

you whose body bristles
with a distant thunder
will miss it, and escape harm.

You who,

slumberous, but sentient,
break through the skin of sleep
to see a hoof kick though a cloud,

pin back the drapes
like insomniacs' eyes

and watch the frantic legs
of the airborne horse flaying
as they carry the dead

join me, and bear witness.

The Wind Phone/Kaze no Denwa

He doesn't want death to end their conversations,
so, after his cousin's passing, he takes a disused phone box
and puts it in his garden.

He talks to his deceased cousin through the broken phone,
tells him how much he is missed.

He isn't the only one who wants to speak to the dead.
After the tsunami, thousands come to make their calls.

School boys scamper up the hill,
phone Grandad to say how big they have grown
since he died.

Even the farmers visit, using their overalls
to mop tears, the black phone
like a charred crescent moon
cupped between shoulder and mouth.

In this glass panel booth full of ghosts,
the sunlight streams through
and the rain slips down like a shroud.

The words do not come down the wire
in his phone box, but travel on the wind.

Callers say to their dead
Is it cold there?
I'll build a house for us again,
in the same place.
Is our son there with you too?
I'm so lonely now.
Will you come home?

A Dream of Fire

Late shift at the diner, soot smuts the window,
a patch of grease resembles a man's face.

Thomas steals a milk bottle, siphons gasoline,
rips cloth to shape a wick

clasps a box of matches
as he follows a stranger home.

Desire is a fire lit under a house,
the inferno his hands,
flames rising like fingers pawing at skin.

His wife lies waiting for him,
wondering why he never touches her,
why his clothes smell of smoke and sulphur.

He creeps back into his house, in the dark,
his fingertips petaled with soot.

She dreams of a wedding dress
made of fire
each dart of fabric is a scorching blade.

First stitches are
red as the rose bud, red as a cockscomb
red as the pomegranate
red as the bloodied face

There are skirts –
hot enough to burn the skin to tinder.

Gold as butterscotch, gold as honey
gold as the pulsing heart of the pyre

Thomas sees flames everywhere;
in the autumn leaf, the river's coruscating tail,
his wife's lashing tongue.

In the morning the sheets look bruised
with charcoal.

Black as a mourning stone
black as a funeral suit
black as a heart charred in the flames.

A Rough Birth

The soil endures a caesarean
before he is lifted out;
he is roseate, as if with blood.

How delicate is this small Cupid
made of bronze,
flaming torch a tiny baton,
wings that could fit a moth.

He is found near a pit of charcoal,
a gift left to the gods.

There is a bow-shaped brooch at the same site,
it would have once pinned a cloak
to keep the cold winds out.

To make this road they slice through the land,
trees are hacked from the earth

wounded roots left clinging to the ground
like children's fingers to their mother's hands.

The scars made by this road will never heal,
and the land is left barren.

I like to imagine Cupid
coming unbidden to an artist's mind,
a red tulip breaking through soil,

then being forged in a fire, his small limbs
welded in a trembling flame.

But not of this rude birth —
the rough hands tearing up Love
from the dark, warm earth.

An Antipathy for the Puppet Man

September, and the robin's song is a crisp melancholia,
an ode to the dying of the light.

Inside the barn, there is puppet play,
Punch's hooked-nose head nodding to the front row,
fierce smile on ruddy skin —a crescent moon
awash in blood.

Outside, our crouched protagonist
deploys his light;
here is a gift for the puppet man – a tupping flame,
a lantern toppled, a flame spills for the barn to drink.

The children are squatting on bales of hay
under a thatch of straw.
At the first flame a boy cries
look how the sun comes closer!

Did this firestarter covet the handling of the string,
the way the puppet master made his effigies dance for him?

Or perhaps he envied Punch, hammer-headed shapeshifter
who outdid the devil night after night,
scarlet-topped mannikin who escaped the noose
and instead hung Satan.

He is acquitted for the fire,
yet later confesses to an antipathy
for the human who dangles Iago from his hand,

tells how he wanted to tamp down
the wonder blazing in an audience's face
feeling all the accolades should be his.

The children are buried together, under a stone
engraved with a blazing heart and angels' wings.

The ghost of a fluting whistle can still be heard,
part boy, part bird,
the robin's sweet song of territory and domain.

Golden Chain

At 13 you lay with him on the grass
looking up at the trees' cascade of saffron fire

as he tells you it is called *Golden Chain*,
turns and touches your blonde hair, smiling.

How could you resist reaching
for the flaxen stalactites
which hung from the tree.

Afterwards sickness,
your body writhing in the night

learning what love is – reaching to the sky,
ripping flowers from the bough
eating hungrily.

Then the sleeplessness, the aching heart.

The Abundance of Samuel Palmer

The visions of the soul, he says,
are the only real sight.

His self-portrait is an inventory of the spirit,
of the instrument it sings through.

His childhood spent in soot-stained streets,
gospel encounters with other painters
lifting him out of the rank pit of the city.

As a boy, visiting Blake, a dying Michelangelo
slumbering in his sun chariot,

returning to his room to thicken watercolour
with gum Arabic to depict a moon flecked
with crow, a scythe in a corn-gold sky

to turn farmers gauzy
as ghosts, luminous as glow worms,
reducing man to a spectral light.

Prodigal artist, Ancient at 20,
singing of Jerusalem,

glowing watercolour gouaches,
gleaming
like the silk inside a magician's cloak.

He is the oracle of blossom,
of the plumed needles of poplar,
the fields of corn, thick as horses' manes,

the bard of boughs heavy with fruit,
weight pulling limbs to the ground.

At the end of his life his son will build a pyre
of his paintings.
All this will be eaten by flame.

But, oh the profusion of the golden apples
before they fall.

Gold Gods Descending
(To Vincent Van Gogh)

The critics speak in jaundiced tones,
sneer that seeing yellow
is a stigma of the mentally unsound,

that your yellow vision means
either damage to the eye
or poison taken in the asylum.

They are unable to separate
the white and the yolk
of insanity and divinity.

Disciple of the sun, you have travelled south:
and your canvases are pure rapture,

your paintings holy with halos,
all things in your eye being sublime.

Your skies spin with coruscating vortices,
bristle with stars,

your fields are oceanic,
shimmering waves of gold
in which a man could drown.

The critics worship their own opinions,
while you rest after painting,
hands steepled in prayer,
dreaming of gold gods descending.

A Conversation with Jung

In sleep, Jung and I converse.
He says
have no doubt, the dead are within us all —
when I dived like a heron into the lake of myself
I met with Elijah and Salome,

and after I had broken bread with them,
the sky burnt through cloud to birth a blue wing
worn on the back of an old man grasping keys.
His name was Philemon.

The next night I dream of Jung again,
and he talks of how Philemon was blessed by the gods,
and lived as closely with his love
as two trees, roots entwined like limbs in a bed.

We walked together in the garden, he says,
talking of the actuality of the soul.

I am tired of the reported speech of sleep
and yearn for Philemon to visit my psyche.

But Jung says
thoughts are not yours to herd,
they just roam across the mind like cattle.

I dream that Jung finds a dead kingfisher,
its wings as azure as Philemon's.

I hold it between my palms
as if one hand were an overarching heaven,
the other the earth below.

An Interior

After Edgar Degas's 1868 painting

What is her name? Her customer doesn't care.
She is now *mon cheri*, or worse, *la Lorette* – a stitch dropped
from the weave of a Paris street.

How snowy her chemise, the only pure thing
in this soiled life.

Her corset lies on the floor –
a wing torn off a *Common White.*

There are closed rose buds plastered upon the wall,
a gloom that the single lamp cannot dissipate,

a narrow bed, blood on the bed head,
splayed legs blocking a way out of the room.

In the silence of the painting we must read symbols –

her sweet face - a moon half eclipsed by darkness,
the shadow he casts making two of him.

At night she remembers her mother's voice,
soft and dusted with love
calling her *Mon biquet, Mon Minou.*

Everything has more than one name.
This scene - some call it **Intérieur**, others **Le Viol.**

After Edgar Degas's 1868 painting **Intérieur/Le Viol (The Rape)**
*Notre-Dame de la Lorette, the setting for the painting, was home to
many women who had fallen on hard times.*

Appetites

Sister, do you remember the birds eating
on the sands? As we got closer we saw
the bold mandibles, their skin-saddle,
the beaks plucking at leftovers,
necks straining as they tore at cold meat.

Do you recall how they immediately took off,
and revolved around us in a circular flight,
as if ring-fencing prey?

The sun caught the underside of their wings
as they hovered above our heads
making a slant crown, a halo.

When they landed again we saw
a hundred bobbing heads, chests pulvinated
with fluffed feathers, bold pectorals,
and I shuddered, remembered
the men who surrounded us
outside the pub, how we stood there shivering

as they strutted. A cold estuary light had glinted
in their eyes, and they flayed their arms
as if airborne.

How luminous the display of appetites,
but how dark in the shadow.

Contrapasso of the Second Circle

Hell wears the Second Circle
like a tree wears its rings.

The First Circle is cold.
In the Second Circle you burn.

In the First Circle you are held for ambivalence.
In the Second Circle you are imprisoned for your passion.

In the First Circle are Virgil and the philosophers.
In the Second Circle – Paris, Cleopatra, you.

In the First Circle they are suspended.
In the Second Circle you are airborne.

In the Second Circle you will be buffered by a restless force.
In the Second Circle you will know the storm.

In the Second Circle
you will get no rest on the wing,
nor will you eat.
In the Second Circle
You will enjoy no embrace.

You will envy the swifts who
sleep in the air,
feed whilst flying,
fuck upon the wind.

Plating the Gods

See how Loki leaps above the waves,
ray-fins glinting,
body quick and agile as an acrobat,
the water his quivering trapeze.

Once deity, magician,
now lithe little fish,
he refracts the moon and sun.

How brave he is to leap.
He wears his scales like armour.

We wait, like bears that hang over rapids,
paws clawing at the air,
mouths like caves

ready to swallow him in one deft gulp
or carry him home limp in our mouths
to be torn apart by our cubs.

Worse, we let him go cold on the slab,
arrange him upon a platter.

In our rough hands
this is where all the gods end up,
sliced, reassembled,
served up as a side-dish.

The Toll

Imagine if this were your brother
broken on the road.

There is the corpse of a jay,
blue patch on his wings brought down
as if a piece were ripped from the sky.

Yesterday we saw a swan,
blood ribboning the broken bones.

After a crow was hit
a fleet of his fellows
circled the body with funeral solemnity.

Too many corpses here to count
and it is still early.

How we can continue our ride
when we pay such a toll for travel?

The bodies of birds are tossed on the road
like small change.

Yet soon other wheels will flatten
these fleshy hillocks,
ensure that our journey home is smooth.

The FBI Agent's love of the Trees
After 'Twin Peaks'

The Agent is in awe of the trees,
conical crowns piercing the storm clouds. 1

His face is beatific as he rolls into the town
and sees the evergreens
enveloped in a winding sheet of mist.

He has answered a call about a killing —
a girl lying dead on the beach. 2

Everyone is under suspicion,
especially those who say they love her.

Found on the body — half a gold heart necklace,
a torn piece of newsprint under a scarlet nail.

It becomes evident that there is a killer who acts at night,
while the wind soughs through the fir trees. 3

Evil leaps from person to person, invisible,
yet the younger sister of the dead girl's friend
still aspires to be a poet. 4

The Agent takes such delight in the trees. 5

After a day's investigations he slugs back his coffee.
He likes it black. 6 and 7

1 *Boughs pointing at the sky in accusation.*

2 *Plastic cocooning her body like mist.*

3 *And the water pours like tossed silk over the rapids.*

4 *And talks of the full blossom of the night.*

5 *As girls lie on slabs like axed silver birches.*

6 *As black as a night without stars.*

7 *As dark as it gets far from civilization.*

Hacked Down
Tilia tomentosa – Petiolaris Weeping Silver Lime

Through my window I watch a man, body bowing
under a weight of wood.
I would compare him to Christ
bearing the cross but he is not the martyr.

> *When first I saw her*
> *I recognised her as a Silver Lime,*
> *she held aloft her dome-shaped crown.*
> *I did not know her to be Weeping.*

He wields his saw
as if he forces hounds at a fox,
Teeth grind and devour until
the hunger is gone.

> ~~*When first I saw her*~~
> *I recognised her as a Silver Lime,*
> *she held aloft her dome- shaped crown.*
> *I did not know her to be Weeping.*

After he has hacked her down
he stretches and yawns,
laughs as his packs away his blades.

> ~~*When first I saw her*~~
> ~~*I recognised her as a Silver Lime,*~~
> *she held aloft her dome-shaped crown.*
> *I did not know her to be Weeping.*

Now her roots snake out from the stump
and a nest lies empty in the dirt.

~~When first I saw her~~
~~I recognised her as a Silver Lime,~~
~~she held aloft her dome-shaped crown.~~
I did not know her to be Weeping

She stood there once,
brandishing heart-shaped leaves.
Now only grief fills the space.
~~When first I saw her~~

~~I recognised her as a Silver Lime,~~
~~she held aloft her dome-shaped crown.~~
~~I did not know her to be~~
weeping.

The Fir Trees are Furious

The trees are indignant that their forests
are the setting for thrillers,
and that it is into their darkness the girls run.

Here they are minding their own business
when along comes a girl, panting and gasping,
perhaps dropping a shoe.

Then come the film crew, the smouldering
actors holding guns, the clustered police,
someone in a white paper suit picking a hair
off bark with tweezers.

This, the Fir Trees say, is a sacred place,
gnarled pillars reaching a blue, basilica sky.

The Wolves feel the same,
being too often blamed
for abductions and attacks
when in fact, they only strike
when they feel cornered.

No one talks about Houses, a maligned
Beech Forest says. The Fir Trees,
trunks furrowed as if with worry, agree.

Doors, they say, should feature
in every thriller, so much horror happens
behind Doors, even the ones the girls
open with their own Keys.

A Doll

The snow looks ghostly in the police photos,
its whiteness almost unnatural
like a false, rictus, grin.

A mother, missing.
'Lynch pin, lodestone, anchor.'
Without her, the daughters are adrift.

Such a diminutive lady, a pocket Venus,
dressed like a little doll,
kitten-heeled boots with tiny buttons.

The daughters are grateful when she is found clothed,
her blouse buttoned right up to the neck.

The female pathologist comments on the shoes,
how they almost fit on her palm

and she remembers her brother,
enraged at her for saying *no,*

taking one of her dolls, tossing it
through the window, so it lay broken,

pearlescent skin and fixed smile
luminous against the black earth,
dainty shoes still fastened on tight.

Rounded Up

They had half- listened up to the point
at which the reporter talked about children
being imprisoned in cages.

Now they switch the car radio off
as it broadcasts a documentary about a Detention Centre.

They park at the edge of the field,
unpack the picnic, the bottle of *Moet.*

The season is opulent,
the grass a cushioned divan.

Across the field a man shouts
as he drives sheep into a lorry.

He whips the air behind the animals
with a stick, as if about to beat them.

The wife averts her eyes,
turns to watch house martins
inscribe their signature in the sky.

The children the government snatched
now sleep in the arms of steel mesh.

Swags of cloud adorn the sky,
the plush hills glisten like satin.

The man is marshalling the lambs.
They huddle together and bleat, as if in pain.

A New Skin

She likes the room where they do Biology,
it is how she imagines the moon to look
up close – the clear white surfaces, the spectral light.

In the morning lesson she learns
how the body rebuilds itself
every seven years or so, how old cells die
and are replaced by new. *A little like leaves,*
her teacher says, *the old ones falling,*
fresh buds breaking out in spring.

School is a *Safe Place*
and she likes the company of her peers,
but even better she likes to be alone,
lying in bed, watching the moon,
nothing, except her sheets, touching her.

To take her mind from memories of the men,
she thinks of what she learnt earlier –
how the body sloughs off dead cells, and hair,
recreates itself.

One day, she thinks,
she will have a whole new body,
one those men have never touched.

The moon has tried to teach her this already.
Watch this, it says and each night
goes into the darkness
then comes out dazzling white again, as if reborn.

Therapist

eighteen months of appointments
and you still can't say the word
or hang your memories on its rough hook

not even the one of the man
flat-palmed and pushing you
back onto the bed each time you tried to sit up

nor the time you woke to a man's weight
your clothes concertinaed

say the word, the therapist says
no need to shy from it but you do

in a documentary years later
a girl talks
of being positioned like a horse

another girl
face eclipsed by shadow
says she was
outside her body looking down

they punctuate their words with pauses
which, like ellipses
leave the listeners filling in the dots

you cannot stop watching
and afterwards you can't get warm

and you shiver and realise that
not one of them used that word
not one of them

Protection

Women have been mauled by wild animals at night.
She reads: *There are many reasons for attack, they include*
Fear-based, defensive and possessive aggression.

Her friends say, *get a big dog to protect yourself from the dogs.*

She gets one from a shelter.
They all look agitated, many of them have sad eyes.
She picks one out that appears vulnerable.

The vet warns her, *don't trust their facial expressions.*
they can turn if they don't get what they want.
She thinks, *he just needs love.*

The one she chooses has a broad jaw, pincer teeth.
On the way home, his stocky frame swaggers.

She takes him with her at night.
The dogs that normally sniff around her
are nowhere to be seen. He tugs at the lead,
salvia drips from his lower lip.

Back home he is constantly hungry and howls for food.
When she goes to bed he paws at the door until she lets him in.

She reads that his type have
a strong desire to control, show a great amount of force,
make much use of their ability to intimidate.

He bites her in the street,
His dangerous behaviour probably comes from your neglect,
her neighbour says.

She reads: *There are many reasons for attack, they include fear-based, defensive and possessive aggression.*

Get another dog to protect you from him her female friends say.

She gets one from a shelter.
They all look agitated, many of them have sad eyes.
She picks one out that appears vulnerable.

Hades' Instrument

Billy-witch, Flying Stag,
you burrow your grub in the stump.

Horse Pincer, Little Oak-ox,
you feast on rotting wood.

Thor's Offspring, The Storm's Insect,
who tamped your thunder down?

Carapace-backed Pugilist,
Bull-Dog with a Shell,
you hold your jaws aloft.

Ebony-Shelled Knight,
Gnarled Nobleman,
you joust your rival in the dark.

Grand Buck Doe, Facecatcher,
you fight the empty night,

Scarce Crabbed Creature,
you scrat in the fallen bark.

Crabbed Composer, Sea God's son
Which nymph drank your bitter song?

Harts' Horn, Hades' Instrument,
crowned with a tiny lyre.

Devil's Mule, Pan's Rival,
where is your music now?

The Feathered Night

The Good Sister is looking for her brothers in the sky.
Because they are the feathered night.

The good sister has walked to the end of the world
to find her exiled brothers and to bring them home.
As she calls to them, her voice finds company.
Because they echo her song.

The Good Sister fears the hunger of the Hunter Moon
and the sun is too fierce, too incendiary.
But the stars guide her kindly, like prophets.
Because they are oracle.

The morning star introduces himself as Lucifer,
angel fallen to earth.
Because in darkness there is enlightenment.

He tells her the brothers circle the battlefield.
Because they feed upon the dead.

Lucifer gives her a bone from a wolf.
But the bone is eaten by the soil.
Because the earth is the mouth of the gods.

The good sister cuts off her finger to use as a key.
Because the tor of love is opened by sacrifice.

The good sister can see her brothers encased in the mountain.
Because the walls of love are lucent.

Her brothers make a nest in her lap.
They tell her she need not fear mortality.
Because they have eaten death.

Poppet

Strange art for a man
but the sharp wands of the needles
suit me well.

I do not paint a picture, *poppet,*
instead I craft the colour and shape of you.
Poppet you grow with each stitch.

I stole a hair as you were sleeping
thinner than a thread, gauzy as a web.
there is scarlet, from where I tore it.

I gave the last one a cross for a heart
stuffed her with straw
cut her stomach, and she bled blond.

Poppet, only the best lamb's wool for you.

I will sew the back of your head
after seeding something in there.

Then I will leave you, little bird,
broken-winged in the chimney stack.

The Accused

(Bridget Cleary's Husband Speaks)

How inflammatory was the fairy in her!
When we poured paraffin on her she took like tinder.

Little *elemental,* she never belonged
in the golden meadows,
instead was born to the wounded fields of night,
prowled skies stubbled with star,
scythed by the crescent moon.

Did she not go selling her eggs near the coven?
Did she not catch the craft as she bartered by the ring?

She cankered with sin like a wormed apple,
fevered, writhed in our bed
so when I woke, there was a changeling
between the sheets.

There are many ways to rid your wife of magic.
When she sickened
we removed her medicine, locked her
in a room, anointed her with our waters.

They speak of guilt but was I the only one
with his hand on a weapon?
Did I dig up the earth alone?
Are mine the only bloodied boots?

There is no dock big enough
for all of us who acted,
and only one judge will weigh all our sins.

A Warning to the Fisher King

Night is a black cape thrown open
to reveal
the white-dove moon.

You toss the net with a sorcerer's flourish.

Fisher King—you try to dredge your heart
from the waters

but what you reach is fathomless,
the waves as sharp as knives.

When you drag your mesh,
minnows dart like impulses you cannot contain.

Broken king,
you lurch with your line,
mistaking your own shadow
for love.

What Price the Catch?

The susurration of the bulrushes,
the ripples through the sedge,

a small voice mimicking the waters' rasping—
an encounter like this doesn't come often.

You cast your shadow, then throw your net
across the water's skin.

When you scoop her from the water
she is light as a minnow,
barely makes an impression on your boat.

Spirit of the waters,
little elemental, in love with the moon,

her eyes - pale planets,
skin gleaming like a mollusc.

This isn't the time for empathy.
What price the catch?

Ignore, when you can, your conscience,
its coin-cold fingers tapping upon your arm.

Harden your heart and begin the long row home,
you will get a good sum for her.

The Milk-White Doo

In a bowl marbled scarlet
she cooks a snow hare.
She cannot help eating.
Soon her husband's dinner is gone.

Greed can stone the heart.
Her boy is in the garden
small enough to broil.

Come here my little son
reared on milk and moon.
You will silver my pot.

Slow cook, flesh
falls away from the bones
like petals from the autumn rose.

The killer's heart petrifies,
whilst this boy's soul is feathered.

He flies above the earth,
a dove the colour of spun silk
singing the song of all that is airborne.

Capturing the Moon

In the inn, men in their mulligrubs,
swill-bellies living off the fiddlers' pay,
blithesome with what spurts from brewers' tap.

In the yard I tip my tankard skyward
to cup the moon.

That night we are all of us gut-foundered,
and here are them that get their grub from smuggling

so when we pawed the surface of the pond
for the drowned cask of looted spoil

we were no worse than scrumpers
plucking fruit that was ripe to fall.

To them *King's Men* who caught us raking
we says we are scooping up the fat coin of the night.

The moon makes lunatics of us all,
they are so easy duped.

These bearsplitters, these dirty beaus
that steal with me, call me *addle pot*,
even *arsworm*, too cackhanded
to carry away the stash.

It's not the brandy I go after,
it's something that falls through a lad's hands
if he hasn't a quill on him,

a planet as slippery and gleaming as a fine soap
scenting the fingers of all who touch it,
richest of all plunder to the scribe.

They leg it, arms full of spirits.
I stay there, ready to bag the moon.

At the Water's Edge

Even if, at the water's edge, he tells you how he wanted to end it all,
and even if the swans glide across the lake, graceful, my friend,

as noble women sweeping into a room,
and even if the sky is lilac, and the moon is rung round with sepia,

and the swan's wings are dappled, like clouds before a moon
and he tells you that because of *this place*, he didn't do it, my friend

and even if the pit waters are cauterised white
by those wings —oyster shells scooping out the dark,

and the scent of the honeysuckle sails across the lake
like a ghost boat, will you still tell him, will you still tell him
how it was the same for you, my friend?

Flotsam

Today the sea broke the back
of another boat.

Is there nothing strong enough
to withstand the weight of water?

Your depression makes you weak
but this morning we walked on the beach,
the sun dull yellow as an old bruise.

As the wind beat the pampas grass
you told me, in a weak voice,

about how tiny plastic toys
washed up on a remote shore
after a boat was wrecked.

We stepped carefully across a line of flotsam;
a broken comb, a pink ribbon, a gold coin
entangled amongst the bladder wrack.

All these things, smashed on the shore
at the whim of the sea.

You told me not to be upset about your sickness.
But tonight I cried
for the little toy ducks bobbing, hollow
on dark waves, far from home.

Trigger Warning available for

sexual violence —
for images of fingers petal-marking a throat,
wrists rung round with red manacles,
flesh marked by leather tongues,
knuckle print
at the side of a head.
Trigger Warning available for
suicide –
for images of M – who stole her husband's pills
texted him to say sorry, just before.
T – a lopped tree
lank against a holding pole, in A and E
telling the nursing staff, he wanted to
get off the ride.
No Trigger Warning available for The North —
for wind turbines, turning like crucifixes,
gulls panning for gold,
ochre sands,
the crumbling lips of the sandstone rocks,
the silver meadows of estuary,
your haunts, ghosted now.
The bullet of hiraeth
maiming you as you walk away from the scene.

What I Learnt from *The Tower*

I visit the tarot reader the day after
we have our final row.
Your words ring and repeat like tinnitus.

If you loved me you wouldn't

When she turns the first card I wonder
is it a crown? A lotus? A little boat?

I don't think you have ever really

The illustration is pure white as divinity,
as a child's clear eye, absence, a pared bone.
She tells me it symbolises an epiphany.

Listen to me, listen to me, I swear you aren't

At the opposite table a woman is told
she will marry soon,
another that *of course* she will have children.

No way, no way will I let you

But my reader turns over The Tower
reveals a building imploding at its foundations
a lightning bolt, a woman blown clear.

You are nothing without

I end things with you, again, shortly after,
dream that night of pale vessels drifting free

as if unmoored, wake with no new gashes
on either wrist.

Dress like that
Loved me
Listening
Go
Me

The Illusion of Touch

On our last day together.
you tell me you *don't feel a connection.*

Before I leave, we walk in the woods.
Your mind is already elsewhere.

The river is about to burst its banks,
the rapids throw themselves over the rocks.

When we return to the car
you close out the weather.
I can still feel the wind on me, I claim.

You shake your head and say
what you think is touch
is merely only the friction of our electrons.

On the train back I marvel
at what magicians our senses are,
tossing down cards that the body will misread.

I think of how contact is really an illusion,
a metaphorical sleight of no hands,

how our atoms repel,
and the repulsion feels like touch.

Later, lying alone in my cold bed
I can hear you say it again,
how you don't feel a connection

and, *'when you thought I kissed you,*
our lips didn't even meet' .

Slim Ghosts

There's a ring of silver birch
behind the fields,
white trunks cauterise the gloaming.

They are a tight family not yet torn apart,
slender sisters, slim ghosts,
wands of the moon.

I stood among them one night to recite a poem
about a father who met death
with bones like the lightest timber.

As I spoke his name I stood on rough twigs,
discarded for being too brittle
for a bed beneath the earth.

How long had I been standing
above the hole,
speaking a language
that those who go below can't translate.

We should leave them alone,
walk lightly over them,
they are with their own
keeping warm, flank to flank,

invisible to us now, and unhearing,
as we call their names out
to an audience of empty air.

Feeding The Invisible

A friend asks if I want the smashed windfall
but I say I do not want storm damage.

Another offers me a ladder so I can reach
into the upper boughs and pluck the rain-swollen.

I will offer *The Invisible* the ripest harvest;
pulvinated raspberries, scarlet finger-thimble fruits,
sleek plums with tight skins, peaches

with feathered flesh, and bright blushing apples –
sweeter after being picked
from a taut stem.

The Invisible only emerges at night
for fears the human will hurt it.

I scatter *The Invisible's* food in the dark woods,
where the only light
comes from the spines of the silver birch,
those thin torches.

This bounty is made as an apology
on behalf of *Man.*

I give this
the way you would offer a lover flowers
when you betray them.

How Gold they are, Before they Fall

In the last days of his life
my father lay on his bed, slender as a sapling.

All through his illness, he was rooted to home,

his energy slowly seeping out.

How luminous he was, in his late season,
his eyes beatific.

The leaves look radiant
as they hang above the dark earth.

How gold they are, before they fall.

A Grief of Trees

Ash Mourning after the death /I imagine Odin, hanging from you. /The runes always in sight/when the world is upturned.

Birch Straight-backed widow, /barked spectre, /ghost.

Chestnut Everyone thinks of the candles, /baby-doll pink, losing their petals too soon. / But what about the boughs/the steady cover you offer.

Elm Sentry of the Underworld, I wanted to join you. /You said not yet.

Hawthorne I cut a bough. /It shredded itself/like mock orange/ on the concrete/as I walked home. /How sacred you were.

Magnolia Late in your life/your blooms were silk cuffs on thin arms/ flesh bowing under the weight of beauty.

Pine You were lofty, an author who sees inside all his characters' souls. /Some nights I aped your omniscience/ by standing on tiptoes /but you looked down on me/spine as straight as a pen.

Sycamore When they axed you I did not see you go down. /I did not see my father die./The hole left is too large to fill.

Tulip Tree He planted tulips in his last year, /their flowers burst from the soil long after he'd been lowered in./ Goblets on flesh-soft stalks/their scent a spilt fragrance.

Walnut Crisp, fallen leaves rock, /like boats with no cargo, /on the sea of his lawn.

Yew To some you resemble death, to me – eternal life. /Look, the moon!/ Hecate looms above us, mocking.

Naming Storms

We hadn't heeded the weather's artillery,
the thunder in our blood had drowned out sound,
but as the sky turned white and rumble to whip crack
we walked out into the storm.

You told me naked we wouldn't get hit,
two pale columns we stood bare
and melting in the heart of it.

All night we were electric, the storm's
rods and tongue;
the tempest was spent before we were.

You are dead now, and storms seem to come often,
yet are no longer ours to own.

Arwen, Anna or Adam,
each tempest is given a moniker.
Yet back then the storms had our name, and no other.

Airborne

The sky will not be empty of acrobats
for long, soon they will come,
ascend the steps into the bright ether.

I watched a girl climb the ladder yesterday,
rise up to a perch at the top,
heard the instructor
tell her to grip the trapeze and leap.

When she swung, the strings seemed invisible,
it looked as if she was hanging from the sky.

That same morning at school a student
dragged herself into class as though her sorrows
were huge stones in her pockets.

She's not the only one round here
to be fixed to the earth by ballast,
but something changes
when they start to write,
their bodies seem airborne.

Yesterday I watched them turn
to crescent moons,
concave against azure.

Those with more experience can turn over
and in on themselves,
subvert their vision
whilst they are up there.

I will never tire of seeing this,
the way these little artists marry the heavens.

The Brightness

The men pour over their hook
and stare at what writhes on it, dying.

I look over their bowed heads,
above their bodies' predatory prayer.

The Full Moon is reflected in the lake.
The dark waters make a mirror.

In a starless sky She gleams
like a citrine crystal
against the black.

How things change,
we used to call Her *Enchantress,*
The Brightness, Hecate.
Farmers harvested by Her,
used Her to illuminate prey.

Once, shortly after my father's death,
I ran on the beach as I was crying,
and She was there – a cut blood-orange
in the blue bowl of sky.

Tonight I am startled by how cleanly
She has sliced the lawn with moonlight.

But still, the men do not look up.

The White Hart

You've been haunted by the white stag shot in the city,

taking a bullet as it ran through the streets.

You dream of its pale flanks,
see it cantering freely through empty streets,
becoming frantic as the traffic began,
and the cars encircle it like hunters.

People tell you it is *just an animal*,
but you know it is a messenger from the underworld,
a disciple of Herne,
animal emblem of spiritual quest,
killed by those who fear a sighting.

You are troubled by the thought of its lifeless
form, white body on tarmac
stark and luminous as the full moon against a night sky.

Rare, a sighting, but we are not surprised
when you send the photo weeks later
of a white hart standing in long grass.

He wasn't afraid, you tell us, of your presence,
in fact, came closer to lock eyes
with you, keep your stare.

His gentle gaze seeming to say that which you often
tell those you love,

that all is well, that the signs are still auspicious,
despite, despite.

A Sea Fret

November, and a mizzle has rolled in with the sea.

The streetlights are stretched moons,
distended crescents bleed white into the miasma.

The dark fur of the bushes
bristle like the tails of startled cats.

How easy it would be to lose our bearing
yet by staying close we act as each other's lodestone.

Our edges blear and meld,
my arm against yours makes almost one limb.

It is as if only we existed,
swathed in the sea's fugue.

Deep in the centre of the fog,
your hair is a web beaded with glinting dew,
a net of crystals, coruscating.

At the heart of the Fret, the day is full of diamonds.

Worm Moon

Tonight is the last full moon of winter.
It rings in the spring.

Some named this moon after beetle cocoons birthed from a tree.

I am looking at old photos.
In one, my sister pushes tiny socks on my feet.

Worm Moon after the insects' nests.

The wool blooms white like pupae.

Some named this moon after the new harvest.

In the next she watches me as I scoop cereal from a bowl.

Plough Moon for the bringing in.

In another she leans down towards me,

Some named this moon after the sweet crop,

our downy heads almost touch.

Sugar Moon for the cane.

There is no colour in the photo. We look

Some named the moon for the new season.

pure white in our nighties, like two

Chaste Moon for the fresh birth of spring.

little larvae, slowly birthing wings.

Nostos

Call this flooded shore
an acre of platinum crop,
a silver harvest unclaimed.

Call these gullies treasure troves,
the liquid bodies of loot,
mirrors for the moon.

Call the gulls your winged-brothers,
let your father's ghost rise with his gold staff,
have him journey with you.

Accustom your ears to the choir of the sea,
attune them to the waves' chorus.

See yourself returned, as hero,
greet all with the one word for stranger and guest.

Recognise this is your homeland,
even when shrouded in Athena's mist.

Return often, if only in sleep
or on nights when you lie restless,
the tidal forces pulling on you.

Know yourself to be shipwrecked
when landlocked.
Call this your Ithaca.

Reading the Tides

At Flow

Is that the ghost of a boat we see, bobbing,
frail as a bird's skeleton?

Closer we see how the craft rides
the swell as if it were on the gust-plucked
Grande Canal, how a branch forms the Bow Iron,
serrated teeth at the rear. Another rises
from the base —a pole surely, a rowing oar —
as if a gondolier were posed upon it,
moving the craft through *The Floating City.*

We can almost see the stripes of a shirt
against the sky, the gilded insignia which twist
and thread along the stern like bladder wrack.

Or is this instead the skiff poled by Charon?
But what does it mean?
That we are can never go back?

Ebb

The sea is out and what we imagined to be
the spectre of a boat
we know now to be an orphaned tree, torso torn
from mother earth, roots ripped and grasping.

There are fraying roots, revealed where the waters
have retreated, a single clod of earth, dark fruit
the sea has not plucked from the bough.

Perhaps this is a tree felled to form *The Masked City,*
offspring of the Cansiglio forest,
ancestor of the subverted wood that birthed *La Serenissima.*

Or maybe we are encountering *Ask* or *Elmba*,
formed from ash and elm, crafted by Odin and others,
tossed into the sea so they would wash up at the shore,
make landfall for the gods.

We stand there, reading the tides, startled by what they reveal.

Could this be the driftwood
that began it all, the wood we came from,
the giving sea showing us, not our ending, but our start?

An Appointment with the Sea

The sea's appointment diary is a blue book
kept in a pale hall. A *Tide Table,*
it includes the times
of High, and Low, predicts the rise and fall
of water levels, illustrates
how the moon makes the sea swell
and flow in, magnified.

A bible of astronomical prediction,
few know even where to find it,
how to read it, yet it is your daily almanac,
your abacus.

You study the numbers to reveal
the engagements of the waves' ushers
and entourage;
the oyster catchers on the shore,
the gulls that ride the currents.

To calculate when birds
will feast on the sands
you subtract an hour from the High,
add an hour after
for the time they may pluck worms as it ebbs.

Sometimes you follow the tabula as writ
and just greet the sea
at its peak, listen to the rhythmic rise
and fall of the water

the song of wind-propelled wave on stone,
sand or marsh grass, watch the gulls soar
above the expression of swell.

First tide is in the early hours,
and you are still turning in your bed,
your slow breath billowing silk,
your soft sighs the sibilance of the spume,

but later, you will be there to see it roll in, blazing,
bearing the sun in its arms,
the way that when you enter a room
you carry in the light to us.

Time and the Harvest

The beach is strewn with flotsam,
remnants of a party,
bladder wrack is ribbon cut from a gift,
discarded mermaid's purses lie empty.

We walk out, late afternoon,
some ancient impulse leading us
across the beach. We are cast in gold
like Corinthian statues.

This is the time of the halted clock.
The wheel has tilted, is stopped as if by stone,
the earth at a standstill
before it leans back into the light.

We are the sun's pilgrims,
compelled to orbit it's circumference
to lean into it, and then away.

Our ancestors would have celebrated Saturnalia
right now, rung the solstice in,
hailed the God of Harvest, of Time.

In other cloisters
the ancients would have raised cups and sung.

I hear their music now,
in the sea's bawdy carousing,
an urgent song of how we must gather up it all up —
time and the harvest —quickly, before it spoils.

All the Fallen Gold

During the pandemic
the galleries close
but what gold we have lost
in the rooms of the *Louvre*
we find everywhere at our feet.

It is autumn, the season for largesse.
The oaks are munificent gods
distributing their wealth everywhere.

Gold where we walk - large palms
of saffron, sun-yellow on grey stone,

fissures and cracks of the dun earth
concealed by the glinting pages
of leaf litter which gleam like lacquer,
cauterise the dark of a November night.

I lift a leaf and hold it aloft.
Here is a token I will take home —
the trees' gilt lamellae,

passport for the dead,
lodestone for the afterlife,
gilded amulet, antidote, talisman for the dark.

I will keep this precious leaf,
and let the winter wear it,
until the underworld gods call for alms.

NOTES

Page 13: Pasiphaë's Confession – As act of revenge, the sea god Poseidon cursed Pasiphae with a passion for a white bull. As a result of this coupling the Minotaur was born.

Page 14: A Riddle – From *The Life Saving Riddle*, a folk story in which a girl escapes hanging by offering a riddle, the answer to which is that she had a dog called *Love* and has taken his skin and turned it to gloves, shoes and rugs.

Page 16: The Painted Hare – One of the exhibits in Boscastle Witch Museum is a ceramic 'hare woman' found under a house. The quote at the beginning of the poem is attributed to Isobel Gowdie, who was accused of being a witch.

Page 24: The Hall of the Chosen Dead has Many Doors – From the Hall of the Chosen Slain of Norse mythology.

Page 26: An Ancestor of Odin – Two ravens flew from Odin's shoulders— Huginn (meaning Thought) flew to the hanged, and Muninn (meaning Memory) travelled to the slain.

Page 27: The Wild Hunt – The Wild Hunt was a skyborne chase led by a mythological figure, perhaps Norse god Odin, and formed of ghostly or supernatural figures. If seen it predicted death or war.

Page 28: The Wind Phone/Kaze no Denwa – A Japanese man assembled a broken phone so he could call his dead cousin, and after the 2011 tsunami thousands came to use 'the wind phone'.

Page 31: A Rough Birth – A small figurine was dug up when an area of historical significance was destroyed due to the building of a new road.

Page 34: Golden Chain – All parts of the common laburnum are poisonous – the bark, roots, leaves and especially the seed pods.

Page 39: An Interior – After Edgar Degas's 1868 painting *Intérieur/Le Viol (The Rape)*. Notre-Dame de la Lorette, the setting for the painting, was home to many women who had fallen on hard times.

Page 41: Contrapasso of the Second Circle – The Second Circle of the Inferno is for those who have let passion rule above sense. From Dante's Inferno.

Page 55: Hades' Instrument – In anger against the musician Cerambos, because of his slanders, the nymphs changed him into a wood-gnawing *kerambyx* beetle': *Antoninus Liberalis*.

Page 58: The Accused – Bridget Cleary's burnt corpse was found in a shallow grave on 22 March 1895. Nine people had been charged in her disappearance, including her husband. A coroner's inquest the next day returned a verdict of death by burning. Her husband claimed he had killed her as she was a 'changeling' and had become a fairy.

Page 62: Capturing the Moon – The story goes that in 1791, a group of smugglers had hidden contraband brandy in a pond. When apprehended they claimed they were trying to scoop the reflected moon out of the water.

Page 67: The Illusion of Touch – The sensation of touch is merely given to us by our electrons' interaction with — i.e., its repulsion from — the electromagnetic field permeating spacetime (the medium that electron waves propagate through).

Page 71: A Grief of Trees – This poem is inspired by The Ogham or 'Gaelic Tree Alphabet'. The 'you' of the poem is the tree.

Page 78: Nostos – Nostalgia, the term we use to describe this longing for what has passed, comes from the Greek nostos, meaning homecoming, and algos, meaning pain. Nostos is the central theme of The Odyssey, the epic following the hero Odysseus as he seeks his way back home from battle in the Trojan War. And his home is *Ithaca*.

Indigo Dreams Publishing Ltd
24, Forest Houses
Cookworthy Moor
Halwill
Beaworthy
Devon
EX21 5UU
www.indigodreamspublishing.com